A SECOND PIANO BOOK

FOR

LITTLE JACKS AND JILLS

By

IRENE RODGERS

Illustrations by

JOANNE WOOD

Ed. 1808

Pictures may be colored with crayons or paint

G. SCHIRMER, Inc.

DISTRIBUTED BY

This book belongs
To

_____

Contents

A Second Piano Book for Little Jacks and Jills

Irene Rodgers

Lambs on the Hillside

Illustrations by
Joanne Wood

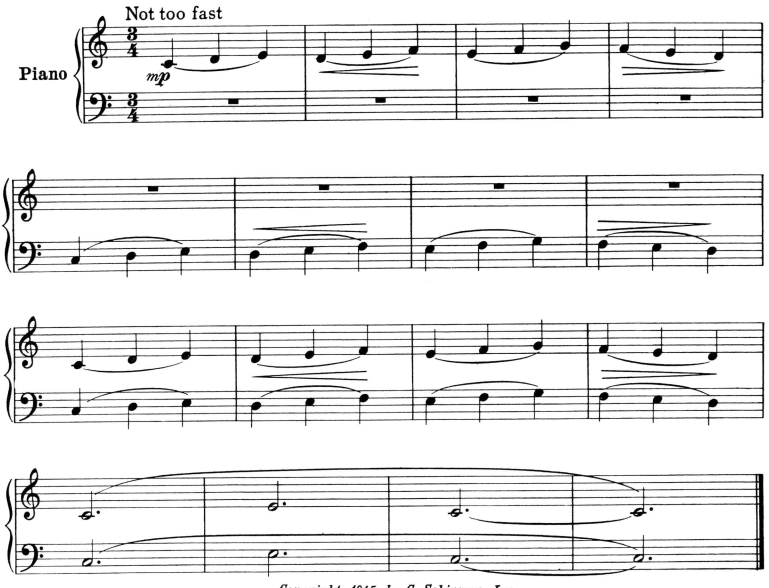

40907 c

Little Lost Lamb

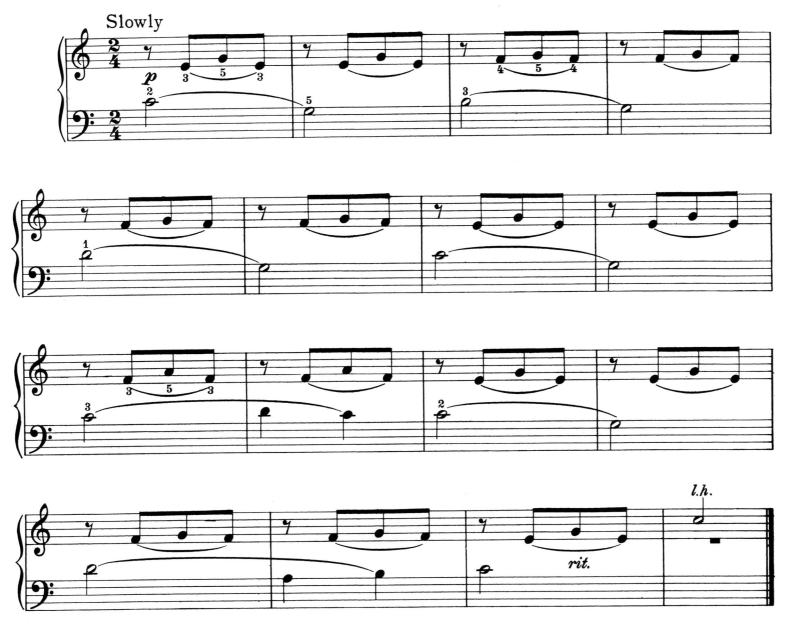

Pussy's in the Well

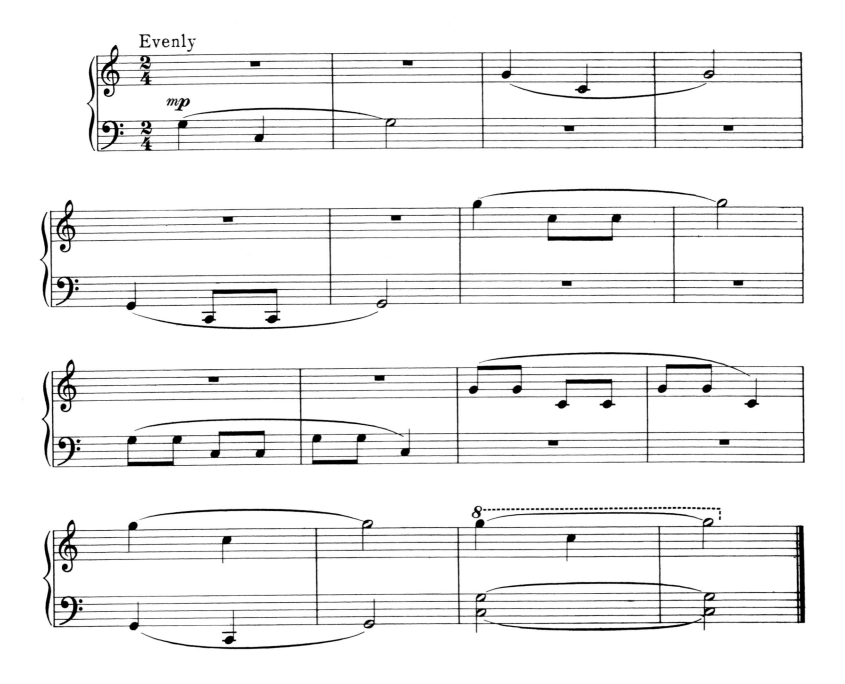

Toy Soldiers on Parade

In March tempo

Waltz of the Dolls

Swans on the Lake

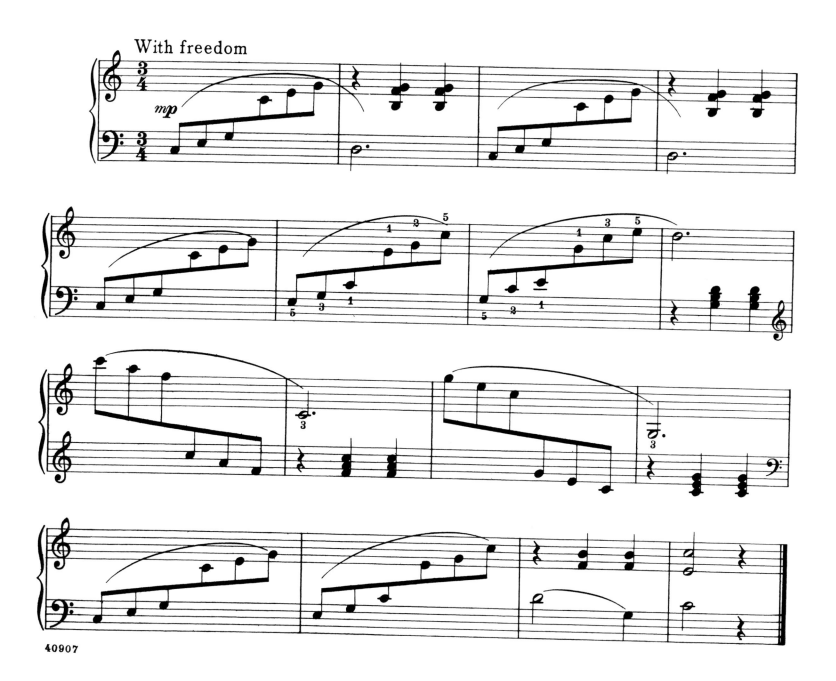

Whirling Pinwheels

A Story of the Wooden Doll

Tom, the Piper's Son

Funny Little Elf Man

There are Hollyhocks in my Garden

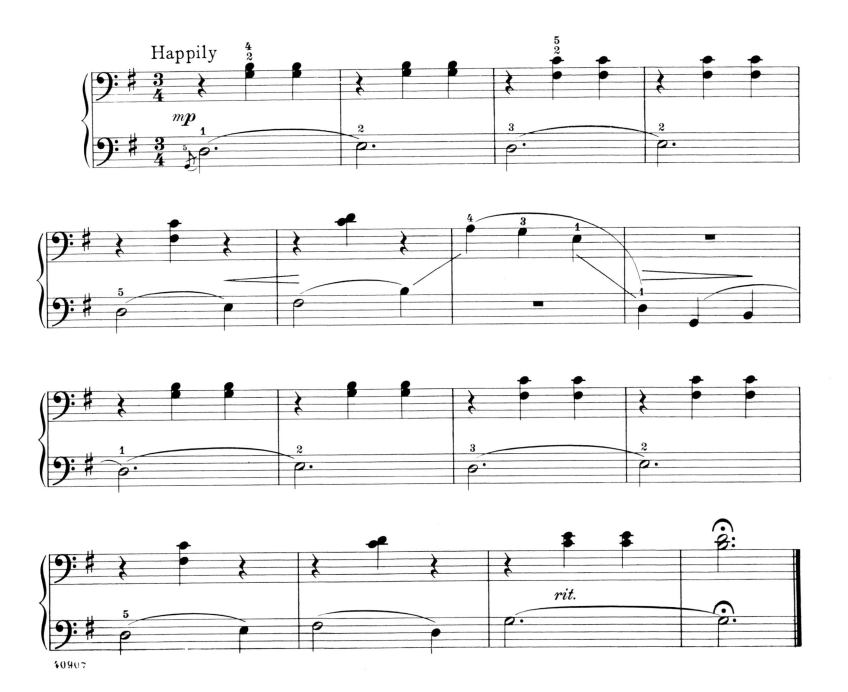

A Strolling Musician

40907

When Stars are Bright

A March with the Scouts

On the Merry-go-round

40907

Scampering Squirrels

The Humming-bird and the Bee

Tiptoeing through the Daisies

Engine Wheels

With movement

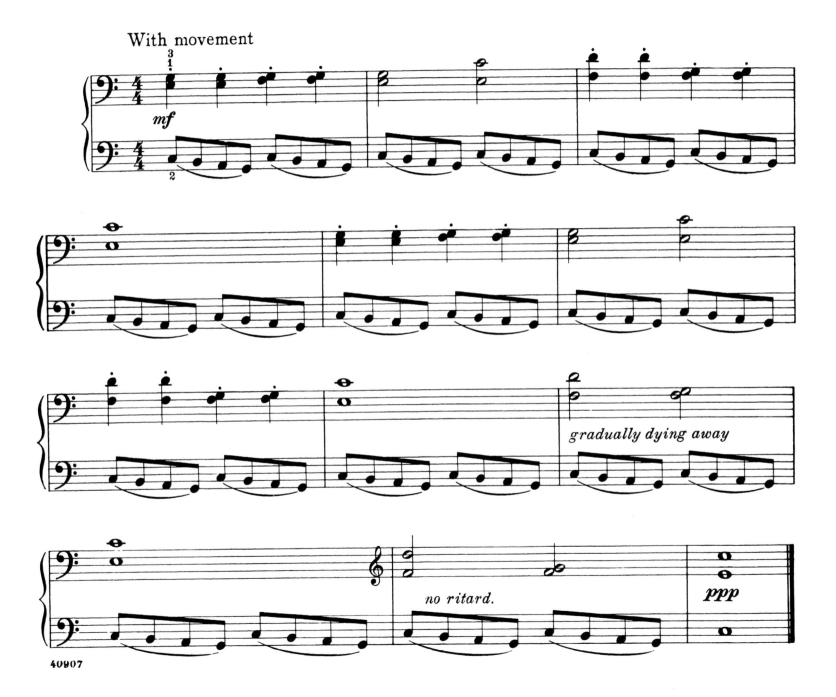

40907

Sea Corals

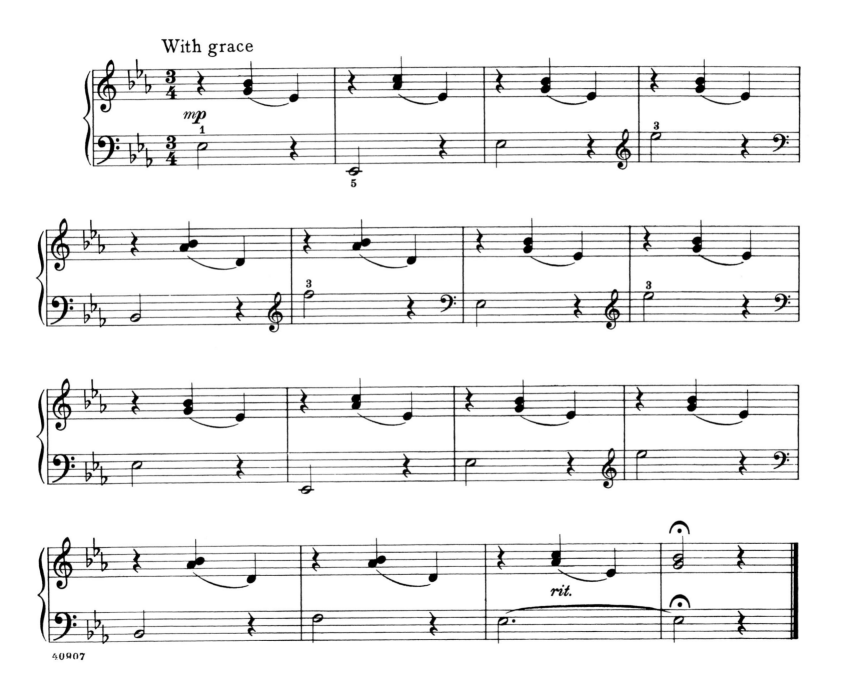

The Flight of the Swallow

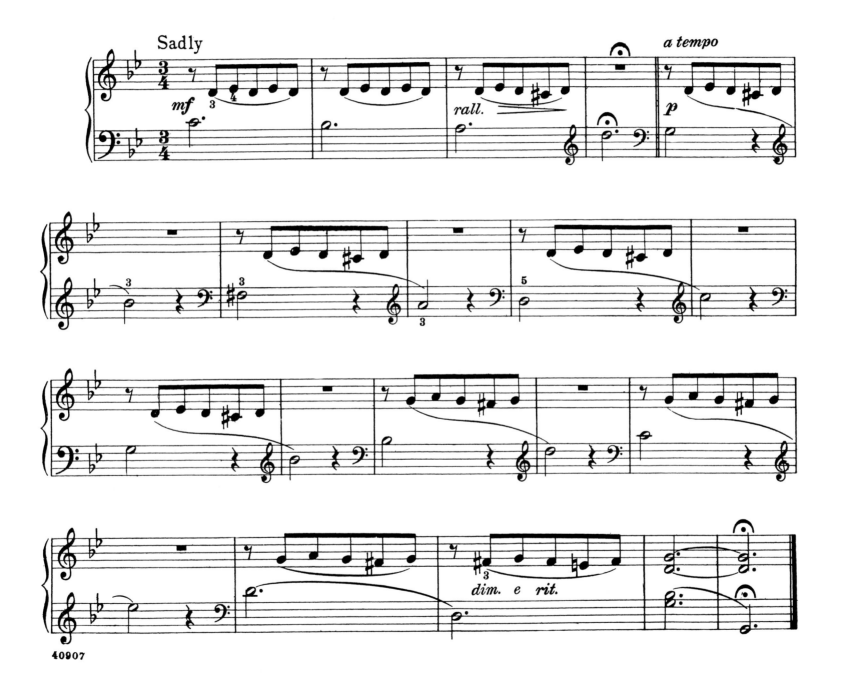

In an Indian Village

Two Little Scale Studies

A Little Tango

Jumping Mud Puddles

40907